Chicken
Poop
In Your
Bowl, II

Jokes, Riddles & 1-Liners
To Lighten Your Load
And Crack A Smile

WRITTEN & COMPILED BY
John M. Irvin

Chicken Poop In Your Bowl, II

John M. Irvin
Lifestyle Enhancement Services, Inc.
Copyright©MCMXCVIII

Printed in the United States of America.

Cover design by Ad Graphics, Tulsa, OK

ISBN: 0-9656428-1-X

"Chicken Poop In Your Bowl, II"
is a trademark of J & C Publishing, Lifestyle Enhancement Services, Inc. and John Irvin, denoting a series of products that may include but is not limited to books, audio cassettes and video tapes.

Published by:

J & C Publishing
P.O. Box 4397
Tulsa, Oklahoma 74159-0397

Order information
To order more copies of *Chicken Poop In My Bowl* or *Chicken Poop In Your Bowl, II*, or to receive a complete list of other products by John Irvin contact:
Lifestyle Enhancement Services, Inc.
by calling toll free:

1-888-997-PHUN

Dedication

This book is dedicated to, first, Cindy, my wife of over eight years. Yes, incredible, eight years. It's the longest relationship I've ever had and the eight years have been an eternity which has flown right by. It has not been easy, but then they tell me that no relationship is easy. The day to day stuff which clouds one's vision of love is not unlike the fleas and ticks and gnats that can ruin any picnic or outing. It is in this area that I am most challenged to remember my own principles, to lighten up and to enjoy each moment by looking for the best, focusing on the positive, remembering to have fun and that love is what really matters. Thank you, Cindy, I think.

Secondly, this book is dedicated to all the fun loving, joke telling people that I meet from day to day in my travels that are always willing to tell me their latest jokes and riddles. Without them, this book would not have been possible.

Thirdly, I am dedicating this book to my mother, Charlene Nan Irvin, for putting up with me my entire life. Anyone disatisfied with any of the jokes in this book can write to her. She lives in Lake Placid, Florida.

Finally, I am dedicating this book to all the brunts of the jokes contained within. And these joke brunts include: chickens, mothers, sons, turtles, farmers, scientists, clones, Tonya Harding, attorneys, criminals, dogs, drunks, Bubbas, highway patrolmen, people from Arkansas, Oklahoma and Texas, cannibals, people who play chess, Americans, the homeless, diets, domestic violence, the English, education, intercultural marriages, geology, work, neutrons, snails, Irish, restaurants and waitresses, bartenders, the Pope, Tiger Woods, Sunday School, government workers (especially elected officials), MacDonalds, men, crime, Mickey Mouse, outdoor toilets, the LAPD, the CIA and the FBI, accountants, Roy Rogers, marriage, traffic accidents, hunters and hikers, people with disabilities, blondes, butchers, Catholics, chief executive officers, insurance companies, alcoholics, Scandinavians, dogs, druggists and ducks, body odor, farmers, first grade, the Mafia, grandpa, fashion, widows, Elvis Presley, ministers, genies, missing persons, babies, fast cars, mopeds, salespeople, the Pink Panther, pit bull terriers, relatives and Rotarians, security guards, kings, accents, scientists, foresters, electricians, and women drivers. Have fun!

Here's The Poop

Introduction

Chicken Poop In Your Bowl, II

Hi, everybody! First of all, I really want to thank you for picking up this copy of *Chicken Poop In Your Bowl, II*. I very truly appreciate it!

Often, people are interested in why someone would take the time and effort to write a book. So I thought that I would take a few moments and describe the series of events that led to the publication of this, and especially, my first book, *Chicken Poop In My Bowl*.

Let's go back in time to a rather dark and rainy day in late autumn. It was the second week of November in 1995, to be exact. I was visiting a dear friend of mine, Bill Monet, who had moved from Tulsa to Asheville, North Carolina a few years earlier.

Bill and I were discussing my rather new career in training and professional speaking. I was working with companies and associations who were interested in improving morale and productivity through providing an opportunity to develop humor skills in dealing with change and stress. The programs were under the umbrella of *Hilarity Therapy®* *Humor Programs* and had been very well received by my clients.

Bill and I were discussing ways in which I could improve my marketing and grow my business. We had been drinking quite heavily.

"You know, Bill," I said, "everyone who does similar work has suggested that I write a book. They say, 'You got'ta have a book!'"

"Well, then," Bill answered, "write one!"

Bill just amazes me. Even through an alcoholic haze he had the ability to reduce a complex problem down into its most simplest form.

"Well, yes, but," I hesitated, "I just don't know what I would really write about. I haven't been dumb struck by any great ideas and I've been thinking about this for quite some time."

"Write a joke book," he said. "You know lots of jokes, and there aren't any great joke books out there. And, you were telling me that people come up to you all the time and complain that they love jokes, but that they just can't remember them."

"That's right," I confirmed. "I always ask them how do they remember anything else, by writing it down. I tell them that they should write the jokes down that they hear. Then they can have a list of jokes, as well as it helping them to remember them."

"Why don't *you* write them down," Bill suggested. "Do a joke book. That way when people say, 'I just don't remember jokes!' you can say, *'Buy this book!'*"

"Hmmmmm," I thought, Bill's idea had merit. "You know, I've thought of a joke book, but then, I thought I would have to make up all the jokes myself."

"No way!" Bill exclaimed. "Write down jokes that people tell you, the one's that you hear. You don't have to make them up!"

"Bill," I cried out, "I think you've got something here. Right now the big thing in books seems to be collections of other people's stories. I mean, look at *Chicken Soup For The Soul*! Those guys didn't make up those stories, they got them from other people, they're other people's stories! I could make a book out of all the jokes that I hear, in fact, I could name the book, *Chicken Poop In My Bowl*! That's hilarious!"

The idea had been born. For the next couple of months, I suggested the idea to others. People laughed when I told them. The idea did, indeed, have merit.

So, I started saving jokes, any jokes and all jokes. I had a big box that I put my jokes in and periodically I would sift through it, weeding out the obscene and gleaming the very best.

In July of 1996, I attended the National Speakers Association Convention in Orlando, Florida. There I had the honor to meet Jack Canfield from *Chicken Soup For The Soul*.

"Jack," I said, "I've had this great idea for a joke book. I want to do a parody of your cover and then call the book, *Chicken Poop In My Bowl*, what do you think?"

Jack said, "Go for it."

"Cool!" I said, "Will you write a foreward for it?"

"Well," he answered cautiously, "I would have to take a look at the book first."

"I can understand that," I answered.

I finished *Chicken Poop In My Bowl* in December of 1996 and the printed copies hit the streets the first week of March in 1997. When people saw it, they did think it was hilarious.

"When are you coming out with another?" people would ask me.

"Hmmmmm," I thought.

1

A Chicken Joke

What do you call a chicken crossing the road?

Poultry in motion.

2

A Snap

The mother watched as her two sons washed the blood from their cut fingers. "I hope you two have learned. Maybe next time you see a snapping turtle, you'll just leave it be!"

"Yes, ma'am," they said, "It really *tortoise* a lesson!"

3

Another Chicken Joke

The farmer came in from outside. His wife was in the kitchen setting the table for the noon meal. The farmer went over to the sink and began to wash his hands. As he rinsed, he remarked, "You know, dear, two of our best chickens have stopped laying."

"Really?" his wife answered, "how do you know?"

"I just ran over them with the tractor," he replied.

4

Athletic Clones

Have you read about those recent cloning activities. A sheep and then a monkey? Well, it seems that they have just made headway cloning athletes (athletes are just short of humans). Their first attempt was to clone Tonya Harding. Yes, they're calling her the *Ice Queen Clone*.

submitted by Ken Harmon

5

Attorneys

Did you ever notice that when someone helps a criminal before and during a crime they are an accomplice? If they help a criminal after a crime, *they're a defense attorney.*

6

Barkers?

Where do you take a dog that barks too much?

A barking lot.

7

Bourbon

The old gentleman walked into a bar and settled on a bar stool. The bartender came over and asked what the old guy wanted.

"Please," he said, "I would like five shots of bourbon."

The bartender poured five shots and set them in front of the senior.

After a bit, the shot glasses were empty and the customer asked, "Sir, could you pour me four more shots?"

The storekeep honored the request, and four more glasses were set in front of the gentleman.

Soon after, those four glasses were empty and the old guy was looking a bit polluted. "Pardon me," he said, "but I need three more shots."

Within a moment, three more glasses were in front of him and he very quickly downed them.

"Okay," he said, "It looksh like. . . I need two more shotsh." By now, his eyes were red, his face was flushed and his speech was slurred.

In a short moment, the bartender was setting those two drinks in front of the old guy. As he set the glasses down, the old guy looked up, and said, "You know, it'sh the funniesht thing. . .but. . . it seemsh that the less I drink, the more drunk I am!"

8

Bubba

The high school had started this "pass or play" program. The big game was coming up this Friday and it wasn't looking good for Bubba, the star player. The Football coach approached one of Bubba's teachers to see if he could get a little help for Bubba.

After explaining the dilemma, the teacher agreed to give Bubba a "special test". The next day, the teacher went to Bubba and he handed Bubba a sheet of paper.

"Bubba," he said carefully, "this sheet of paper has your test questions on it. Go home, study the answers and you'll pass. Then you'll be able to play on Friday."

The test time came.

The teacher asked, "Bubba, name the days of the

week that begin with the letter T."

"Hmmmm. I know that one, hmmmm, it's today and tomorrow," said Bubba.

"What?" the teacher exclaimed, "Well, how many seconds in a year?"

"Twelve," Bubba answered, this time without any hesitation.

"Twelve?" the teacher asked in dismay, "How do you get twelve?"

"January 2, February 2, March 2. . . ," Bubba continued.

"OK, OK," the teacher said. "How many d's in Rudolph the Red Nosed Reindeer."

"One hundred and twenty," came a quick reply.

"How the heck do you get one hundred and twenty?!" the teacher cried out.

"DaDa Da da da da da da da da da da. . ."*

(Sing to the tune of Rudolf)

9

Bubba, Again!

Then there was this other Bubba. He was driving down the highway in his big delivery truck. A state trooper pulled out behind him and was heading in the same direction. They hadn't traveled too far, when the Bubba pulled off to the side of the road, and got out of his truck handling an old tire iron.

The state trooper could see him as he passed the delivery truck and then continued to watch from his rearview mirror.

It seemed that this good old boy walked to the back half of his truck and proceeded to beat the heck out of it with the tire iron. After a few moments, he walked back, hopped into his cab and continued driving.

The state trooper thought this was a bit curious, so he, too, pulled to the side and waited for the delivery truck to pass. He then pulled back out and began to follow the Bubba and his delivery truck.

Just a couple of miles down the road, Bubba pulled his truck off the road and again, jumped down out of the cab with that tire iron. He went to the back of the truck and smacked it a few times. Jumped back into the truck and took off.

The highway patrolman watched and wondered. "The guy's breaking no laws," he thought to himself, "but this sure is curious business." He continued to follow and to his wonderment, the same procedure was repeated every few miles. He could control his curiosity no longer. He put on his flashing lights and pulled old Bubba over. He approached the delivery truck, greeted the old boy and asked in his usual manner to see his license and registration.

The patrolman then asked the old boy about his unusual behavior.

"Dang," Bubba said. "You see, my load limit is two tons and I'm carrying four tons of parakeets back there. I figure, I've got to keep half of 'em in flight, or I'd be in trouble."

10

Bubba, And Even Again!

Good old Bubba walked into the Food Court at the upscale mall. He looked over the menu and then approached the lovely young blonde behind the counter.

"May I take your order?" she asked.

"Yes'm," he said. "I'd like a quickie."

The young lady looked down at the display and then looked back up at Bubba. "That's pronounced *'quiche'*," she answered.

11

Bubba, Once Again!

Good old Bubba. He sure has trouble with the ladies. The other night he was out with his friend, Joe. Joe never has any problem with the ladies. Bubba asked him what was his secret.

Joe replied, "Well, the trick is to talk with 'em. You got'ta pretend that you're interested in hearing about them and their problems. You don't have to have any answers at all, all you got to do is listen. And, once in a while, give 'em a good compliment."

"Hmmm," Bubba thought, "that don't seem too hard."

Bubba was off. Joe watched from the other side of the room and he saw old Bubba sidle up next to this gal. Things seemed to be going real smooth and then, all of a sudden, Joe watched as he saw that gal wallop Bubba right across the face. Dang near knocked him down.

Bubba came back on over to Joe. His head was hanging low.

"What happened?" Joe asked. "Things looked like they were going pretty good."

"They were," Bubba answered. "I was just a listenin' to her talk. I was noddin' my head and from time to time I would say, no kiddin'. Things were goin' great. And then, I remembered what you said about givin' 'em a compliment from time to time. So I said, 'You don't sweat much fer a fat one.' That's when she let me have it!"

<u>12</u>

Bubbas

These two bubbas were driving along in their semi-trailer when they came to an overpass. There, painted on the cement, they read: *Caution: Low Clearance 11'4"*. They got out of their cab and measured their rig. It came to 12'2". They looked at one another puzzled for a bit, wondering what to do. Then the one said to the other, "Hey, there's not a cop in sight, let's go for it!"

13

Cannibals

Did you hear what the one cannibal said to another?

"I never met a man I didn't like."

■ ■ ■ ■ ■ ■ ■ ■

Then there were the two cannibals that were sitting by the fire. "I sure hate my mother-in-law," said the first.

"So try the potatoes," offered the other.

■ ■ ■ ■ ■ ■ ■ ■

Did you hear about the one cannibal that asked his dinner companion, "Aren't you through eating yet?!"

"Hey," the second one answered, "I'm on my last legs now."

Once upon a time a cannibal canoed over to a neighboring island. On this island the price for people was $5. However, the price for politicians was $50. The visitor was shocked.

He asked, "How come the price for politicians is so high?"

"Come on," exclaimed the local, "have you ever tried to clean one?"

■ ■ ■ ■ ■ ■ ■ ■

Then there was the poor guy who got captured by cannibals. They kept him in this bamboo cage. Every day, they would poke him with their spears and use his blood to wash down their food.

One day the guy got really upset and he called over the chief. "Listen," he said, "I don't care if you kill me. I don't care if you kill me and then eat me. I'm just tired of getting stuck for drinks."

14

Chess Fans

What do you call a bunch of chess aficionados standing around in a hotel lobby chatting with one another?

Chess nuts boasting in an open foyer.

submitted by Cynthia John

15

Chick, Chick

Then there was the case of the poor mother hen who observed the undisciplined behavior of her youngest chick with obvious disapproval. "If your father could see you now," she cackled disgustedly, "he'd turn over in his gravy."

16

Communicating In This World

What do you call someone who speaks three languages?

Trilingual.

■ ■ ■ ■ ■ ■ ■ ■ ■

What do you call someone who speaks two languages?

Bilingual.

■ ■ ■ ■ ■ ■ ■ ■ ■

What do you call someone who speaks only one language?

An American!

17

Dating

You know what the best thing is about dating a homeless girl?

You can drop her off anywhere!

18

Diet

At a wellness conference in New York not long ago, a dietitian was addressing a large audience.

"There are long term consequences for our diets," she stated. "The food we eat today determines our health tomorrow. With what many of us have put into our stomachs throughout our lives, it is surprising that some of us have lived as long as we have. This speaks of the awesome ability of the body to rejuvenate itself. But what we eat today does determine our health tomorrow. It will catch up to us. We need to take a serious look at the dangers of our diet. Of course, we need to reduce our red meat consumption. We want to reduce our intake of pork, fried foods and those foods high in fat and sugar. We should consider the pollutants in our drinking water. But most of us our totally unaware of the dangers of one food substance. Would anyone like to venture a guess as to what I am referring?"

A gentleman raised his hand.

"You, sir," the dietitian pointed, "please, would you tell us your thought."

"Wedding cake?" the man ventured.

19

Domestic Violence

What do you say to a woman with two black eyes?

Nothing. You can't tell her nothing. I already told her twice.

submitted by Vicki Adelman

20

Duh!

A Brit was traveling through the heartland of the United States. He was doing some shopping at one of the local markets when old Bubba overheard him talking.

"Hey there, buddy," Bubba asked, "where are yew from! I shore do like yer accent!"

"I'm from Britain, actually," the traveler answered.

"Britain!" Bubba continued, "Where the heck's that?!"

"It's an island," the Englishman explained, "an island off the coast of Europe."

Bubba looked surprised. "You shore do speak good English fer a European!"

21

Duh, II

That same Brit was traveling through Arkansas by bus when he began a conversation with one of the locals seated next to him. She let him know that she had been born and raised up there in Arkansas, and he responded in kind by saying he was from Britain.

"And what kind of language do they speak over there in Britain?" she asked him.

"We speak English," the gentleman responded.

"Well," she continued, "how long have y'all been speakin' English over there in Britain?"

The mind of the Englishman turned over and he thought of all the great orators and writers of English; Churchill, Tennyson and then back through the ages to Shakespeare and Chaucer.

"I do believe," he said thoughtfully, "I do believe that it must be about 700 to 1000 years."

"Huh!" the lady muttered. "Here in Arkansas, we've been speakin' English all along!"

22

Education

Education is what allows you to get into more intelligent trouble.

23

G is for Groan

Did you hear about that Saudi woman who married that Spanish gentleman? They had two sons, identical twins. They named one, Juan, and the other, Amahl.

They looked so much alike that *if you've seen Juan, you've seen Amahl!*

24

Geology Humor

What did the leaf say as it became fossilized?

I'm impressed.

■ ■ ■ ■ ■ ■ ■ ■

What did one layer of rock say to the layer of rock beneath it?

I'm getting sedimental over you.

submitted by Andrew Weston

25

Hmmmmmm.

You know, a train station is where a train stops. A bus station is where a bus stops.

At work, I have a work station.

26

How Much?

A neutron walked into a beer joint.

"A beer, please," the little neutron asked of the bartender.

The bartender drew up a cool one, topped it off, and set it down in front of the little guy.

"How much will that be?" asked the neutron.

"For you?" answered the bartender, *"No charge."*

27

Huh?!

One New Year's Eve, at a very ritzy bar, a bartender looked down and there before him sat a small snail.

"Excuse me, sir," said the snail, "could you please serve me a vodka tonic?"

"I'm sorry," he said, "but we don't serve molluscs."

"But why not, sir?" asked the tiny creature.

"We just don't! Now get the heck out of here. Now!" yelled the barman excitedly. And with that, he took his thumb and forefinger and flicked the little fellow out the door.

The next New Year's Eve arrived. Just before midnight, the barman looked down and there he saw the very same snail from the year before.

"Hey!" asked the snail, "What did you do that for?"

28

Irish Bean Soup

Why are there only 239 beans in Irish Bean Soup?

If there were one more, it would be *too-farty*.

submitted by Susan King

29

Law Briefs

What's the difference between a dead dog in the road and a dead lawyer in the road?

There are skid marks in front of the dog.

■ ■ ■ ■ ■ ■ ■ ■ ■

What do you have when a lawyer is buried up to his neck in sand?

Not enough sand.

■ ■ ■ ■ ■ ■ ■ ■ ■

Do you know how to save a drowning lawyer?

Take your foot off his head.

What's the difference between a lawyer and a bucket of feces?

The bucket.

■ ■ ■ ■ ■ ■ ■ ■

What is the definition of "a shame"?

When a bus load of lawyers goes off a cliff.

■ ■ ■ ■ ■ ■ ■ ■

What is the definition of a "crying shame"?

There was an empty seat.

■ ■ ■ ■ ■ ■ ■ ■

What do you get when you cross the Godfather with a lawyer?

You get an offer that you can't understand.

■ ■ ■ ■ ■ ■ ■ ■

Why test rats when there are so many attorneys around?

Some things a rat just won't do!

■ ■ ■ ■ ■ ■ ■ ■ ■

Where can you find a good lawyer?

In the cemetery.

■ ■ ■ ■ ■ ■ ■ ■ ■

What's the difference between a lawyer and a vampire?

A vampire only sucks blood at night.

30

Lemonade

It was a very hot day and the thirsty and tired businessman was walking past a small restaurant when he noticed the sign in the window stating, "Lemonade, All You Can Drink For $1".

This sounded like just the ticket to the parched guy, so he went in and sat down at the counter. He quickly ordered a lemonade.

The waitress brought it over, set it down and said, "That'll be a dollar."

Our hero reached into his pocket, pulled out a crisp one dollar bill and plunked in onto the counter top. He picked up the glass and quickly drained it down his gullet. He set the glass down, called to the waitress and ordered another lemonade.

The waitress brought over a new glass, as she set it on the counter, she said, "That'll be a dollar."

"Wait a minute," the frustrated and still thirsty patron complained, "your sign said, all the lemonade you can drink for a dollar."

"That's right," the young lady responded. "And that's all you can drink for a dollar!"

31

Leroy

There was this guy, Leroy. He was drinking in a bar while the President was giving an address on the TV in the background. Leroy looked at the bartender and said, "Yep, me and that guy, we go a long way back, we used to hang out together and do a lot of fun things back before he became the president...".

The bartender looked at him and told him he didn't believe him. Leroy asked for the phone, he dialed the White House and asked for "Mr. President". He talked for quite a while, he was joking and laughing and presently he handed the phone to the bartender. The bartender was flabbergasted! He was talking to the President of the United States.

A couple of weeks later, Leroy came back into the bar. They were watching a golf tournament and Tiger Woods was taking a putt.

Leroy said, "Yep, Tiger and I, we go way back."

The bartender said, "Leroy, I admit, you knew the President, but I don't believe that you know Tiger."

Leroy reached behind the counter and grabbed the phone. He dialed and started talking, he was referring to the person on the other end as 'Tiger'.

The bartender took a glance at the TV screen and sure enough, Tiger was talking on a cellular phone. He waived into the TV camera and Leroy handed the phone over to the bartender. He was talking to Tiger Woods.

Another week went by and Leroy came into the bar once again. This time, the Pope was making a televised address.

Leroy said, "Yep, when we were little, the Pope and I were always into mischief."

The bartender did not believe Leroy. "You are surely kidding, this time!" he shouted. "Certainly, you can't know the Pope, too!"

"Yep, I've know him since we were five," Leroy smiled.

After a lengthy argument, the two decided that there was only one way to settle this. They decided that they would fly to Rome and visit the Pope, in person. The two men got on the phone to a travel agent and within a week, they were on their way.

In Rome, they found themselves standing in the crowd at the Vatican. They were watching the Pope as he finished that day's Mass. Leroy worked his way through the crowd, and up the steps. The bartender was totally amazed to see him shake hands with the Pope and then the two immersed themselves in conversation, a conversation that appeared to be that of long time acquaintances.

After a bit, Leroy and the Pope came out into the crowd. Leroy wanted the Pope to meet the bartender.

They were surprised to find the bartender sprawled flat out on his back, passed out, cold. Leroy got some water and began to splash it into the bartender's face. Finally, the bartender began to come around.

"What happened?" asked Leroy.

"Well," the bartender said, "while you were talking to His Holiness, some little old lady tapped me on the shoulder and wanted to know, "who was that up there talking to Leroy?'"

32

Lessons From the Lamb

The new Sunday School teacher was trying to impress upon her young students the need for staying within the teachings of their faith. She believed that she had come up with the perfect analogy.

"You see, children," she began. "The little lamb didn't understand the dangers of straying from the flock. Although she was warned over and over by her parents and by the elders of the flock, each day, the little lamb would venture to the very edge of the flock. She found it to be exciting. One day, she went just a bit too far away and the wolf swooped down on the little lamb before she ever knew what happened. He carried her up into the rocks and the brambles where the others could not help and there, he killed the little lamb and ate her."

The children looked at the teacher in awe.

"Now," she continued, "that wouldn't have happened had the little lamb stayed with the flock, would it?"

"No," cried out little Johnny, "she would have been eaten by us!"

33

Light's On

How many federal employees does it take to change a light bulb?

Sorry, that item has been cut from the budget.

■ ■ ■ ■ ■ ■ ■ ■

How many bureaucrats does it take to change a light bulb?

Two. One to screw it in and one to screw it up.

■ ■ ■ ■ ■ ■ ■ ■

How many law-makers does it take to screw in a light bulb?

Four hundred and sixty-two, twelve to investigate the President's involvement in the failure of the old bulb, twenty-three to deregulate the light bulb in-

dustry, sixteen to cut funding for alternative light-ing, thirty-four to cut the tax rate on light bulbs, fifty-three to design a block grant so the states can change the bulb, forty-one to talk with defense con-tractors about night-vision gear instead, and two hundred and eighty-three to pass a law making it illegal to discuss screwing bulbs on the Internet!

34

MacDonalds

Do you know why MacDonalds came up with the triple cheeseburger?

Research showed that Americans were living too long.

And, I understand that MacDonalds has opened up their first restaurant in India. Now this didn't make any sense at all to me at first. I mean, they don't eat beef in India. But then I learned that they were making the burgers out of lamb.

I guess they're calling them, Big Ma-a-a-a-acs.

35

Making Things Right

A Bible study group was discussing the unforeseen possibility of their sudden death. The leader of the discussion said, "We will all die some day, and none of us really know when, but if we did, I'm sure that we would all do a better job of preparing ourselves for that inevitable event."

Everybody nodded their heads in agreement and a few spoke up with, "Amen!"

Then the leader said to the group, "What would you do if you knew that you only had four weeks of life remaining before your death, and then the Great Judgment Day?"

A gentleman said, "I would go out into my neighborhood and my community and minister the Gospel to all those that I met who have not yet accepted the Lord into their lives."

"Very good!" said the group leader, and all the group members agreed, nodding their heads, yes, that would be a very good thing to do.

One woman spoke up enthusiastically, "I would dedicate all of my remaining time to serving God, my family, my church, and my fellow man with a much greater and earnest conviction."

"That, too, is wonderful!" the group leader commended her, and all the group members agreed, nodding their heads and saying, "Amen!"

One gentleman seated far in the back finally spoke up and very loudly he said, "You know what I would do? I would go over to my mother-in-law's house for the four weeks. I would go over there and stay with her."

"Is your mother-in-law ill?" asked the leader.

"No," the man answered.

"Is she in need of some sort of assistance?" someone else asked.

"No," he answered again.

"Does your mother-in-law have the need to be saved?" another questioned.

"No," he replied once more.

Everyone was puzzled by this answer. Finally, the group leader asked, "Why would you go over to your mother-in-law's home?"

Then the gentleman smiled and said, "Because, that would be the darn longest four weeks of my life!"

36

Men Bashing

Why do doctors slap babies' butts right after they're born?

To knock the penises off the smart ones.

■ ■ ■ ■ ■ ■ ■ ■ ■

How can you tell if a man is lying?

His lips are moving.

■ ■ ■ ■ ■ ■ ■ ■ ■

How are men and women alike?

They both distrust men.

■ ■ ■ ■ ■ ■ ■ ■ ■

Why is psychoanalysis quicker for men than for

women?

When it's time to go back to childhood, he's already there.

■ ■ ■ ■ ■ ■ ■ ■

What do you call a handcuffed man?

Trustworthy.

■ ■ ■ ■ ■ ■ ■ ■

What does a birthday, an anniversary, and a toilet all have in common?

Men always miss them.

■ ■ ■ ■ ■ ■ ■ ■

How are men like commercials?

You can't believe a word they say.

■ ■ ■ ■ ■ ■ ■ ■

Why are men like blenders?

You need one, but you're not quite sure why.

■ ■ ■ ■ ■ ■ ■ ■ ■

What is the only time a man thinks about a candle-light dinner?

When the power goes off.

■ ■ ■ ■ ■ ■ ■ ■ ■

What do you instantly know about a well-dressed man?

His wife is good at picking out clothes.

■ ■ ■ ■ ■ ■ ■ ■ ■

How is a man like the weather?

Nothing can be done to change either one of them.

■ ■ ■ ■ ■ ■ ■ ■ ■

What is the difference between a man and child-birth?

One can be terribly painful and sometimes almost unbearable while the other is just having a baby.

■ ■ ■ ■ ■ ■ ■ ■ ■

What is the difference between a single 40-year-old woman and a single 40-year-old man?

The 40-year-old woman thinks often of having children and the 40-year-old man thinks often about dating them.

■ ■ ■ ■ ■ ■ ■ ■ ■

Women dream of world peace, a safe environment, and eliminating hunger. What do men dream of?

Being stuck in an elevator with the Double Mint Twins.

■ ■ ■ ■ ■ ■ ■ ■ ■

Why don't men often show their true feelings?

Because they don't have any.

■ ■ ■ ■ ■ ■ ■ ■ ■

What's the difference between government bonds and men?

Bonds mature.

■ ■ ■ ■ ■ ■ ■ ■

Why are all dumb blonde jokes one-liners?

So men can remember them.

37

Miami Vacation

An "out of towner" parked his car in a particularly crime-ridden part of Miami, he boldly walked up to two young street toughs sitting on a nearby wall. They were sipping something from some brown paper sacks.

"Excuse me, lads," he interjected, "if I park my car here overnight, do you think it will still be here in the morning?"

"Say, what?" one answered. "If you parked your car anywhere in Miami, it would still be *here* in the morning."

38

Mickey

When Walt Disney was just a young lad, he went to work for a small company as an illustrator. He was very good and very well liked. After a few months, however, Walt became bored and began to make mouse sketches. He always used this one particular notebook and whenever he had any extra free time, he would open this notebook and begin to sketch.

After some weeks of this, his co-workers began to be irritated. He never socialized with them as he had previously, but was constantly making those mouse drawings. He was obsessed!

One day, a fellow employee decided that he would pull a small prank on Walt. When Walt had excused himself from his desk to go to the bathroom, this particular guy stole over to Walt's desk and took the notebook. He hid it beneath a stack of old newspapers that were to be thrown away.

In a short time, Walt returned and it wasn't very long at all before he noticed his missing sketches.

Walt was incensed! He ran through the office screaming, "Where's my mouse pad! Where's my mouse pad!"

And, now, of course, you know the origin of, 'the mouse pad'.

39

Mixes and Matches

Then there was that Unitarian boy who married that Amish girl. He drove her buggy!

■ ■ ■ ■ ■ ■ ■ ■

Have you heard about that couple who got married in the nudist colony? They wanted everyone to be sure who the best man was.

■ ■ ■ ■ ■ ■ ■ ■

Old Bill and Trisha have never stopped feuding. And they've been married now for over forty years. Why, even the day they got married, you could tell there would be trouble. They were standing at the altar and when it came to the part where the pastor asked for the vows, old Bill said, "I do," Trisha shot right back, "Oh no, you don't!"

■ ■ ■ ■ ■ ■ ■ ■

I read in a book the other day that girls always marry men like their fathers. No wonder so many mothers cry at their daughters' weddings!

40

Modern Facilities

There was a Native American family that lived on a reservation. They were very poor and had no paved roads, there was no electricity, no indoor plumbing. The medical services were scarce. It was not a happy place.

One of the tribesman knew that the only way out of this dilemma was through education. His oldest son was very bright and, indeed, he even enjoyed school. The father felt that this young man should be the first of his family, in fact, the first of the tribe to attend the university.

The tribesman scrimped and saved and learned of some grant monies, the boy studied hard and qualified for some scholarships. Through both of their long efforts the boy was admitted to the university.

The boy studied hard and did well. After four years, he was awarded a diploma with honors. He now held a degree in electrical engineering.

His homecoming was quite festive. The clan had cooked for days and people came from hundreds of miles to honor the lad for his achievements.

That night, as the festivities were winding down, the boy had to make his way to the bathroom. The path was dark and it had been so long since he had been home, he was not completely sure of the way. And, after being so long in the city, he seemed not to see as well in the dark, either. He was tenderly trying to find his way when he stumbled hard over a rock and fell to the ground. He fell hard and bruised and cut his body and his head. He became angry.

For the first time in his life, he was angry over the conditions in which they lived, the poverty, the lack of electricity, indoor plumbing, the seemingly hopeless state. He vowed to do something to correct the situation.

The next morning, bright and early, he was up and working on his first project. Before the end of that day, the young lad had installed lights all along the path that led to that outdoor latrine as well as the latrine itself. It was a magnificent job and he was very proud of his work.

This was the very first Native American who ever *wired a head for a reservation!*

41

Now Hear This

Then there was the poor guy with two red and burned ears. He went to his doctors office and the doctor asked him what had happened to his ears.

"I was ironing my shirt and the phone rang," the little guy said. "But instead of picking up the phone, I picked up the iron and stuck *that* to my ear."

"Goodness, man," the doctor exclaimed in disbelief. "But then, what happened to your other ear?"

The patient replied, "Well, whoever it was, called back."

42

Police Work

Did you hear about the recent exercises that were held by the Los Angeles Police Department, the Federal Bureau of Investigation and the Central Intelligence Agency? It seems that the three organizations were in a conflict. Each was claiming to be the very best at apprehending criminals. They agreed to an exercise which they felt would prove who was the best. They enlisted the aid of an independent research firm who released one particular rabbit into the forest. The test was to see which of the three organizations could find the rabbit the quickest.

The C.I.A. went into the forest. They recruited and placed animal informants throughout the area. They questioned all the plant and mineral witnesses. They offered a very lucrative reward on any information leading to the apprehension of the rabbit. After three months of extensive investigations, they concluded that rabbits do not exist.

The F.B.I. went in. After two weeks with no leads they burned the forest, killing everything in it, including the rabbit. They made no apologies. The rabbit had it coming.

Finally, the L.A.P.D. went in. In just two hours, they came out with a bear. The bear was bruised extensively, he had two broken front legs. Blood was pouring from his nose and several cuts about his head.

The bear was yelling, "Okay, okay, I'm a rabbit, I'm a rabbit!"

43

Quickies

What is worse than being with a fool?

Fooling with a bee.

■ ■ ■ ■ ■ ■ ■ ■

Why did the father call both of his sons Ed?

Because two 'Eds are better than one.

■ ■ ■ ■ ■ ■ ■ ■

Why do you suppose Cinderella was kicked off of the football team?

Because she kept running away from the ball.

■ ■ ■ ■ ■ ■ ■ ■

What clothes do lawyers wear in court?

Lawsuits.

■ ■ ■ ■ ■ ■ ■ ■

Have you heard what the sea said to the shore?

Nothing, it just waved.

■ ■ ■ ■ ■ ■ ■ ■

What did the jack say to the car?

Can I give you a lift?

■ ■ ■ ■ ■ ■ ■ ■

What are hippies for?

To keep your leggings up.

■ ■ ■ ■ ■ ■ ■ ■

How do you stop a herd of elephants from charging?

Take away their credit cards.

■ ■ ■ ■ ■ ■ ■ ■

What do accountants use for birth control?

Their personalities.

44

Roy's New Shoes

Dale Evans went into town to do a little bit of shopping. While in a local department store she noticed a wonderful pair of brown oxford shoes that she felt would be a nice gift for her husband, Roy Rogers. She had never seen Roy in a pair of shoes before. He had always worn boots. "Won't he be surprised," she said to herself.

Well, Roy was surprised. He was delighted! He loved the new shoes. He put them right on and looked in the mirror. "Boy, howdy," he thought, "these sure look good!" He went into town and showed them all around in the coffee shop. He went to find Pat Brady to show him the new shoes.

Pat was off doing a little hunting, so Roy set off up the trail to see if he could find him. A couple of hours later, he and Pat were standing around admiring those oxfords on Roy's feet.

Back home, Dale was upset. Roy came in and tracked mud all over the place. While finding Pat, he had gotten those shoes dirty, muddy and grimy!

"Roy!" Dale screamed, "You get those shoes off your feet right now! Go set them outside the door! I've got enough to do without having to clean up after you!"

Roy promptly removed the soiled footwear and put them outside.

The next morning, Roy sprang from his bed and ran out to get those new oxfords, clean them off and head on into town. He opened the door, reached down and. . .they were chewed to pieces! "What! They're destroyed!" he thought. "How can that be!"

Then, his head cleared and his eyes focused on some large cat tracks. A mountain lion had come in from the hills that night, found the shoes, chewed them up and trotted back up into the foothills. "Dang! That cat won't get away with this," he said to himself. He quickly dressed, saddled up Trigger, loaded up his Winchester and headed off into those hills following the obvious sign that cougar had left.

Several hours later, down he came. Dale was looking out the kitchen window as she saw the sun glare off the muzzle of his rifle. As he came closer, she could tell that a large mountain lion lay dead across the back end of Trigger, draping lifeless on either side of the horse.

She ran out to greet the successful avenger, and quickly burst into song:

*"Pardon me Roy, is that the cat that chewed your new shoes?"**

**(Sing to the tune of Chattanooga Chew Chew)*

45

Socrates on Marriage

By all means marry, if you get a good mate you'll be happy. If you get a bad one you'll become a philosopher.

46

That's What Some Call It

What do you call a lifestyle that excludes the possibility of having sex?

Marriage.

47

The Accident

Old Mrs. Finley passed right on through a red light and was involved in an accident.

Although she seemed fine, the ambulance thought it prudent to take her to the hospital and have her thoroughly checked out and examined by a doctor.

When she returned home, her face was ashen and she appeared visibly upset. Her 37 year old son noticed her appearance and asked what was wrong. He was very concerned.

"Son," she answered, "I've got a flucky. I don't know how long I've got left. I'm just so worried and so afraid!"

"What!" exclaimed the son. "What on Earth is a flucky?"

"I don't know," she said, "all I know is that I was

in a car accident today and when the doctor looked me over, he told me that I've got a flucky. I'm so scared."

She was nearly in tears, and the boy was so confused, he thought that the best thing to do was to call the hospital and speak to the doctor himself.

"Oh, yes," the doctor remembered, "the woman who was in the automobile accident this morning, she sure got off lucky!"

48

The Aggies

Some while back, I was down in Austin, Texas. I was sitting in a restaurant sharing a booth with two other guys. We were having a great time, we had finished our lunch and now we were telling jokes to each other. I got into some Aggie (Texas A&M) jokes and I just didn't realize on what thin ice I was skating! Before I knew it, a guy was tapping me on the shoulder. It was the guy from the next booth and he had overheard some of these jokes. He was very big and very offended.

"Listen, jerk," he started, "I don't appreciate you making fun of my school, and by golly, now you're going to pay!"

The big cowboy pulled out a razor! I couldn't believe it! They were only jokes! I was really scared, I mean terrified! That is, until I realized there wasn't any place for him to plug it in!

submitted by Sam Sikes

■ ■ ■ ■ ■ ■ ■ ■

Did you hear about the great Texas and Oklahoma war?

Yeah, a group of Texans came to the border and threw over a bunch of dynamite.

The Oklahomans just laughed, lit it and threw it back.

49

The Amphibious Philosopher

In the words of the greatest Bullfrog, "Time's fun when you're having flies!"

■ ■ ■ ■ ■ ■ ■ ■ ■

And do you know why lobsters don't share?

Because they're shellfish!

50

The Balloonists

Then there were those two guys who had set out in a hot air balloon to cross the Atlantic Ocean. After several days in the air, the one said to the other, "You know, I think that we had better lose a bit of altitude. Get a little lower so we can find out where we are."

They began to let out some of the hot air and the balloon began to descend. Before long they were below the cloud cover. They could not make out any land marks and so still, they had no idea of where they might be.

The two adventurers continued to descend and in a short period of time, they could make out automobiles traveling. Soon they could distinguish individuals walking about below. The one fellow said, "Hey, let's get above that guy down there, perhaps he can tell us where we are!"

In moments, they were over the figure's head and the one shouted down, "Hey, buddy! Can you tell us where we are?"

The gentleman on the ground looked up, he hesitated for a moment and then shouted out his answer, "Sure! You're 100 feet up in the air in a balloon!"

The two men looked at one another. And then, the one said to the other, "that guy must be an attorney! The information he gave us was 100% accurate, and totally useless!"

51

The Bear Hunt

One clear day, a beautiful springtime day, a Czecho-slovakian was walking along an Idaho county road. He wasn't paying much attention, but gazing at flowers and looking up into the clear blue sky. He didn't notice the approaching grizzly bear that had turned onto the empty road behind him.

The grizzly bear had awakened and stirred not too very long ago. He was quite hungry from his long winter nap. He caught the scent of food from the hiker's knapsack. He attacked.

The nearby townspeople found the remains of the devoured Czechoslovakian and were horrified. So soon in the year they had to deal with a killer bear. They put together a posse which included many of the prominent local business people, the grocer, the sheriff, and also, the car dealer and the banker, to name but a few.

They tracked the killer grizzly for three days. Then the bear's tracks were joined by those of another bear. Now they followed both sets of footprints.

Along toward sundown they followed the two giant sets of tracks into a box canyon. Surely, they had those bears trapped. Excitement and tension grew among the anxious men.

Then, suddenly, there they were! Both bears standing high on their rear legs, growling and snarling in a fearful and threatening manner. The men were frozen for a terrifying moment and then took aim. But wait! Which bear to kill? Only one of the fierce animals deserved "harvesting". The other was innocent.

The men hollered to the sheriff, "Which one? Which one?"

"I don't know!" the sheriff called back. "I just don't know! All I know is the one on the left is a male and the other is a female! But I don't know which one killed that poor hiker!"

With that, the banker stood up, took aim and shot. The deadly bullet met it's mark and the bear on the left toppled and fell. The other bear turned and fled up the steep mountain side.

"But how do you know that's the one?" the sheriff asked the banker.

"Well, in my twenty years of banking, the Czech is always in the male!" he replied.

submitted by Katie Spaetti

52

The Bell Ringer

Once upon a time in the middle ages, there was a small community that was graced by a fantastic church with a beautiful bell and tower. All of the goings on within this township was monitored by the ringing of this great bell.

It so happens that one summer the church was in the need of a new bell ringer. The church had put out notices and the Father was interviewing the prospects.

This one particular day a man came for the interview. This man had no arms. The Father asked him, "Sir, how do you intend to ring the bell when you have no arms."

The man answered, "Father, it is not a problem, the Lord has blessed me with a solid head. I can ring the great bell by running across the platform and striking it with this hard head of mine. Please, let me demonstrate."

So the two went into the tower and climbed the stairs until they reached the bell.

The applicant said, "Watch this!"

He lowered his head and charged the bell. As he reached a few feet from the bell he leaped, striking the bell fully with his noggin. The great bell rang, and it was of a beautiful tone. Magnificent! The bell ringer repeated his performance. Fantastic! And once more, but, this time as he ran forward, he stumbled, lost his balance and plummeted from the tower to the courtyard below.

The Father was aghast! He ran down the steps to find the broken body of this young man. As he feared, the man was dead. A crowd gathered, and in a short time along came the local constable.

"Who is this man?" the constable asked.

"I don't know," sighed the priest, "but his face rings a bell!"

53

The Bell Ringer, Too

Once again in the middle ages, there was the same community that was graced by a fantastic church with a beautiful bell and tower.

It so happens that one summer the church was still in the need of a new bell ringer. The church had put out notices and the Father was interviewing the prospects.

The week before, a man with no arms had fallen from the tower and was killed. This particular day another man came for the interview. This man, too, had no arms.

"Father," he said, "my brother left our village last week and had come for this job. My family is very poor and we are in desperate need of work."

The Father told the man of his brother's demise. "I am sorry, my son, but your brother is dead."

The man answered, "Father, then let me try, the Lord has blessed me with a solid head, and I also have great balance. I can ring the great bell by running across the platform and striking it with my head. I will not fall. Give me a chance, I beg of you!"

So the two went into the tower and climbed the stairs until they reached the bell. The man said, "Watch this!"

He lowered his head and charged the bell. As he reached a few feet from the bell he leaped, striking the bell fully with his noggin. The great bell rang, and it, too, was of a beautiful tone. Truly magnificent! The bell ringer repeated his performance. Fantastic! And once more, but, this time as he ran forward, he, also, stumbled, lost his balance and plummeted from the tower to the courtyard below, just as his brother had fallen.

Not again! The Father ran down the steps to find the broken body of this young man. As he feared, the man was dead. A crowd gathered, and in a short time along came the local constable. "Who is this man?" the constable asked.

"I don't know," sighed the priest, "but he's a dead ringer for his brother!"

54

The Blonde

Just the other night, a friend of mine, Dave, was out clubbing. He, being single, is on a constant search for that right female, that one woman who could become his life's partner.

He happened to be sitting next to a beautiful blonde and they had begun that infamous ritual of getting to know one another.

"Where's your family?" Dave asked.

"Oh, they live in Ohio," she answered.

"Do you have any brothers and sisters?" Dave proceeded.

"Oh, yes! I have two brothers," she continued, "one is 18 and the other is 25. Their names are Sammy and Alfred."

"Really," Dave asked. "Who is the oldest?"

"Duh!" came the answer, "the 25 year old, of course!"

55

The Butcher

A man walked into the butcher's shop. He looked around and then baited the butcher. I bet you a hundred dollars that you can't reach that meat up there on that top shelf.

The butcher thought for a moment and replied, "No, the steaks are too high!"

<u>56</u>

The Candle

Mrs. O'Donovan was walking down O'Connell Street in Dublin, and coming in the opposite direction was Father O'Rafferty.

"Hello," said the Father, "and how's Mrs. O'Donovan, today? Didn't I marry you and Mr. O'Donovan two years ago?"

"Yes, that you did, Father."

"And are there any little O'Donovans yet?"

"No, not yet, Father, not yet," she said.

"Well now, I'm going to Rome next week, and I'll light a candle for you."

"Thank you, Father, that's very kind, Father." And away she went.

A few years later they met again.

"Well now, Mrs. O'Donovan," said the Father, "how are you today?"

"Oh, very well," she replied.

"And tell me," he said, "have you any little ones yet?"

"Oh yes, Father. I've had three sets of twins, and four singles, ten in all."

"Now isn't that wonderful!" he said, "How's your lovely Mr. O'Donovan?"

"Oh," she said, "he's over visiting in Rome to blow out that bloody candle!"

57

The C.E.O.

This gentleman had just been hired as the new chief executive officer of a great high tech firm. It was a Fortune 500 company. The C.E.O. who was stepping down met with the new man on a number of occasions to get him up and running. On their last meeting, the old guy took the new guy aside and presented him with three envelopes. The envelopes were numbered 1, 2 and 3.

"When things get rough, open the first of the envelopes. The answers to your problems lie within. There isn't anything, no problem that can't be solved by the contents of one of these envelopes," he assured the new, and yet nervous executive.

Things went along very smoothly, for the first six months, but then, sales took an awful downturn and the new C.E.O. began taking an incredible amount of heat. The board was looking for answers and the stockholders were complaining. Just about at his wits's end, the new guy finally remembered the envelopes. He went to his drawer and took out the first envelope. He opened it and the contents read, "Blame your predecessor."

The new C.E.O. called a press conference and he tactfully laid the blame at the feet of the previous C.E.O. Satisfied with his comments, the press, the board, the investors and Wall Street, all responded positively. Sales picked up and stock rose. This problem was soon behind him.

A year later, the company again began to experience a great dip in sales, combined with serious quality problems. This time the C.E.O. very quickly recalled the envelopes and as soon as he started receiving complaints and inquiries, he immediately went to the drawer and pulled out the second envelope. The message read, "Reorganize." This he did, and the company quickly rebounded.

After several profitable quarters, the company again fell on difficult times. The phone began to ring, the board was concerned and the stock began to take a significant dip. The C.E.O. went to his office, he closed the door, he went to his desk

and opened the drawer containing the final envelope. He opened and read: *"Prepare three
envelopes."*

58

The Claim

A farmer was suing an insurance company for a settlement on a bodily injury claim. It seemed that the farmer had been traveling along in a horse drawn wagon, while his dog was sitting next to him. Then, suddenly, from the other direction, a car traveling at high speed came swerving toward them. The car crashed into the horse drawn wagon, hurling the entire mess into a ditch. The insurance refused to pay for the farmer's injuries.

The attorney interrogated, "From the officer's report at the site of the accident, you stated that you were, indeed, not injured, that you suffered from no injuries, and yet, now, you claim that you were injured and are seeking major restitution. Please explain how that might be."

"Welp," the farmer began, "I had been lying down in that ditch for some time. My dog was lying some ways away. I couldn't see him, but I could hear him whimpering. I could hear my horse breathing heavily and he, too, was moaning in his way. I could tell by the sounds that they were making that they were mighty hurt, too. The deputy pulled up in his squad car. I could hear him get out and he walked over to my horse. He apparently saw that the horse was hurt bad. He took out his revolver and shot the horse. He walked over to the dog. I guess he saw that the dog was hurt bad, too. Because he put a round in my dog. Then he came over to me. Under the circumstances, I figured it was best to say that I was okay!"

59

The Company Picnic

The disgusted wife looked on in tremendous dismay as her drunken husband made a terrible fool of himself at the company picnic. She was finally approached by one of the top executives in the firm.

"Your husband certainly seems to drink excessively," he said to her.

"Well," she mused, "You'd drink too, if you had his problem."

"Really?" the executive responded. "What is his problem?"

"He's an alcoholic," she answered.

60

The Cross-Eyed Cow

Olie and Sven had this cross-eyed cow. They were saddened each time they looked at the poor thing and so one day, they decided to see if they could do something to help. They went to the nearby veterinarian's office and explained the situation to the vet.

"Oh, sure," the vet said. "That's an easy thing to fix. In fact, you can do it yourselves. Let me explain it to you."

Olie and Sven listened very closely and went home to their farm very thrilled and excited at the prospect of uncrossing the beast's visual receptors.

As they reached the farm, they drove straight up to the barn where the sad cow stood. Olie went into the barn and brought out a six foot length of soft rubber tubing. Sven stood at the front of the cow, holding it's halter and looking it straight in it's crossed eyes. Olie took the tube and went around to the rear of the cow. He lifted the cow's tail and with some initial effort began to slide the rubber hose up into the cow's rectum. Sven held the cow steady. Then, with the hose in place, Olie began to blow steadily into the end of the tubing. He blew harder and harder, and sure enough, as he blew, Sven noticed that cow's eyes beginning to straighten. Olie blew and blew, and those eyes got straighter and straighter, but just as they were close to being right, Olie ran out of air. He pulled back his head to catch his breath and those eyes snapped right back into their original cross-eyed position. Olie and Sven groaned and moaned with their frustrated efforts!

"Olie," Sven said, "How about you coming up here? You come up here and you watch the eyes, and let me come back there and give it a try, eh?"

"You betcha'," Olie agreed.

So the two exchanged places. Sven went to the rear of the great milk provider while Olie went to the front to hold the halter and to watch the progress of the big brown crossed eyes.

As Sven got into position, the first thing that he did

was to grab hold of the hose. He pulled it out, turned it around and began to slide it back in.

Olie looked around from the head of the cow. "Sven!" he cried out. "What do you think you are doing?"

Sven replied in a deliberate tone, "You don't think I want to put my lips where you've had your's!"

submitted by Lawrence Zipp

61

The Dog

A butcher was leaning on his counter towards the close of the day when this little dog entered the shop with a basket clenched between his teeth.

"And now, what's this all about?" the butcher asked out loud.

The pup knocked the basket sharply into the butcher's shins.

"You little mutt," the butcher said in an angry tone. He reached down to smack the little dog and then he noticed a note and a twenty dollar bill in the basket.

The note asked for 3 pounds of his best ground beef and a pound of sliced smoked turkey.

The butcher figured that he could make a bit of a scam. He went to the counter and reached for the dried up stuff that had been sitting out all day. The dog glared and began to growl menacingly at him. The butcher, quite startled, looked up at the little dog. He then thought better and went to the refrigerator and measured out the best ground beef. He weighed out about 2-1/2 pounds, and then he dropped his thumb in on the scale. "Who'll know?" he thought.

Again the dog growled, and barked sharply.

"Okay, okay," the bartering butcher said, as he measured out the last half pound. He wrapped it up and dropped it in the canine's carrier.

He watched the dog closely as he went for the turkey. He noticed that the young pup's eyes followed his every move. As he started to reach for the unsmoked variety, the dog barked again, warning him of his choice.

The butcher took out the smoked turkey and sliced out a pound of the meat, not daring to attempt to stiff the clever canine again. He wrapped it neatly and dropped it into the basket with the ground beef. He took the twenty and put it into the register.

The dog snarled.

"Okay, okay," the meat meddler maintained. He took out the appropriate change and dropped it in the basket along with the receipt.

The pup left the store.

Now the butcher had become quite intrigued so he called his young assistant from the back to watch the place while he tailed the faithful pet. He followed him down one street and over two. The dog went into a high rise tenement and the butcher followed. The dog went to the elevator, pushed the "up" button. As the doors opened the dog entered and pressed the "door open" button while the butcher came in behind him. The capable canine set down the basket and reached up with his nose and pressed the button "12". The elevator ascended and the door opened when the two reached the twelfth floor. The pup picked up the basket and left the elevator, followed, of course, by the veal vendor. They continued down the hallway. The dog stopped at a door and then began to bang softly on the door with the basket.

Soon the door opened and the dog went inside.

The meat man complimented the owner of the little

pup. "That is a darn smart dog you have there," he said.

The owner replied, "What do you mean? This is the third time this week he's forgotten his key!"

62

The Drugstore

Then there was the guy who walked into the drugstore, went up to the pharmacist and asked, "Say, do you have any acetylsalicylic acid?"

"You mean, aspirin?" the pharmacist asked.

"Yeah," the man explained, "I can never remember the word for it!"

63

The Duck

A duck waddled into a pharmacy. He waddled right up to the pharmacist and asked, "You got any corn?"

The pharmacist said, "No, we don't have any corn."

The next day, the same duck waddled in and asked the pharmacist again, "You got any corn?"

The pharmacist shook his head and said, "No, I told you, we don't have any corn."

The next day the duck came in again. He waddled up to the very same pharmacist and asked, "You got any corn?"

The pharmacist responded, this time quite angrily, "No, I told you we don't have any corn and if you come in here and ask again, I'm going to nail your beak to the floor!"

The next day, the duck waddled in and approached the pharmacist.

The pharmacist looked down with a scowl.

The duck asked, "You got any nails?"

The pharmacist answered, "No."

The duck said, "You got any corn?"

submitted by Mitchell Godi

64

The Elevator

The doors to the elevator opened and the smartly dressed business man entered. The doors closed and the elevator began its ascent to the upward floors. The gentleman began to sniff the air repeatedly as he became aware of a most unpleasant odor.

"I'm afraid to say that someone's deodorant has failed," he said with an air of certainty.

He looked around. As he did, he noticed that the others in the elevator had all moved to a side leaving one particular and a rather shabbily dressed man to himself. All eyes gazed on this poor chap.

Realizing that everyone was looking at him, the guy spoke up, "Listen everyone, it can't be me. I'm not wearing any deodorant!"

submitted by Everett Williams

65

The Farm Boy

This young Midwestern farm boy decided one day that he was going to leave the farm and join the Army. He told his ma and his pa of his plans and although they were disappointed, they wished him their best. He went down to the local recruiter and signed up.

The time finally arrived for his first leave. He went home to visit his folks.

"How do you like it?" his father asked him.

"Pa," he said, "It's great! The food's real tasty, the work's not too hard and best of all, they let you sleep real late!"

66

The First Day

It was the first day of kindergarten class and the lovely young teacher was giving instructions to all the little kids. She was telling them about how they need to stay in their chairs unless they had permission, she was telling them about how they should raise their hands when they wanted to contribute to discussion. She was letting them know about staying in line, being quiet and all those kinds of orderly things. Finally, she said, "Now, if you need to go to the bathroom, you need to raise your hand and hold up two fingers."

"How's that going to help?!" little Billy shouted.

67

The Godfather

The big gangster boss was in his office with his three adult sons. He pulled out a .38 handgun from his desk, he stuck it up to the youngest one's head. After a few moments he asked, "Okay, kid, what does two and two add up to?"

The youngest son thought, he thought very carefully and finally he answered, "Five!"

The boss then moved on to his oldest son, he held the .38 up to this son's head and asked, "Okay, kid, what does two and two add up to?"

The oldest son answered without taking any time at all, "Six!"

Then the father moved along to his other son, he pointed the gun right between the boy's eyes and he asked, "Okay, kid, it's your turn, what does two and two add up to?"

This boy looked his father straight in the eyes, without hesitation, he answered proudly, "Four!"

The father pulled the trigger. The gun went off and with quite a mess, that son was dead on the floor.

The other two boys were astonished. "Pop," they cried out, "Why did you whack him?"

The father was looking down at his slain son. He looked up at the other two boys and said, "I had to. He knew too much!"

68

The Grandpa

Old man Smith was being visited by his son, his son's wife and his little granddaughter, Julie. Julie came up to the old man and said, "Grandpa, can you make a sound like a frog?"

"Sure, I can, Julie," he told her.

"Well, Grandpa, are you sure?"

"Of course, I'm sure, Julie," he promised.

"Grandpa," she continued, "will you please make a noise like a frog, please?"

Grandpa was beginning to wonder what this was all about. "Julie," he asked. "Why do you want me to make a noise like a frog?"

"Well," she said, "I heard Grandma say that when you croaked, we were all going to go to Florida!"

69

The Great Jean Heist

Did you hear about that truck load of Calvin Klein Jeans that was hijacked? The hijackers are described as being armed, white, in their mid-twenties and extremely trendy!

70

The Hat

A woman brought an old picture of her dead husband to the photographer. In the picture, the old man was wearing a hat. The woman wanted to know if the photographer could remove the hat from the picture.

"Of course," he assured her. "With the new computer technology I'll be able to fix the photo right up. You won't be able to tell that there was ever a hat in this photo."

She was convinced. "All right," she said. "Please do it! When do you expect to be finished?"

"Well," he thought for a second, "I'm sure that I can have it ready for you the day after tomorrow. One question, though, can you tell me which side your husband parted his hair?"

"I forget," she answered. "But you can see for your-self when you take off his hat!"

71

The Hunt

The big game hunter decided that he would return to Africa for more trophies. This time, his wife insisted that he take her with him. He agreed. In fact, he thought that it would be a grand thing if she could develop some of the thrill of the hunt that he experienced. Perhaps in the future, she would be more understanding of his outings. To encourage her more, he bought her a beautiful high powered rifle with a grand telescopic site.

Off they went. They were gone for three weeks and when they returned, the hunt's results were less than satisfactory for the game hunter. He had only taken a few species of deer. The big trophy it seemed, belonged to his wife. She had bagged a wonderful mature lion with an amazing mane.

Their neighbor was quite impressed. "Did she get it with that magnificent rifle you bought her?" he asked.

"No," the hunter confessed. "She hit it with the station wagon."

72

The King

I am always amazed at how some of the most famous and creative stars of the entertainment world got their starts.

Elvis Presley was a young truck driver, fresh from the farm when he first cut a record. In those days he never went anywhere without being accompanied by his pet pig, Elmo.

Every one of his songs were ballads about different aspects of life with Elmo. They were together all the time and Elvis was so very fond of the small beast. There were those who tried to tell him that he would never be a star unless he dropped the pig and began to sing of another subject. It just proves how wrong people can be. In order to succeed, we must follow our own path, and our own heart.

One day Presley turned up at the studio without Elmo.

Everyone in the studio was stunned and they all asked, "Where's Elmo? Where's your pig?"

Elvis was grief stricken. Tearfully, he explained that his pickup had broken down on his way into town. He had fashioned a leash out of some hemp rope for Elmo and they started to walk the rest of the journey into town.

They were following the dirt and gravel road which traveled along a small river. This river was, on this particular day, quite swollen from a torrent of rain the day before. They came to a place where the road ran closest to the water and little Elmo broke free of his tether and rushed to the bank in order to devour some garbage that the current had swept ashore.

Elvis called to Elmo and chased after him. The little pig dodged his efforts, and slipped in the wet grass. Elmo was then whisked away in the rushing and swirling torrents.

Elvis ran along side the water's edge, watching as little Elmo was tousled to and fro, his little head barely keeping above water. As Elvis ran on, he watched in horror as the little pig tired, his head sinking below the water's surface. As though in a nightmare, the water gave up Elmo's little body another couple of hundred yards down stream. When Elvis reached his beloved pig, the life was gone from the soaked carcass.

He cried aloud as he finished the story to the studio's workers.

"Maybe now you can sing about something else?" they asked.

"To heck I will!" he shouted.

He retired momentarily to the bathroom. He came out moments later, still red-eyed and mournful, with some words scribbled down on some paper hand towels. He went forth into the studio and struck the first chord of one of the songs which made him so great, and sang *"You ain't nothin' but a drowned hog!"*

73

The Last Call

The young and dedicated pastor went to visit an elderly and dying man. The old man had already done his time in the hospital and had requested that his last days be spent at home. He had no desire to spend hours, days or maybe months hooked to life support equipment.

He knew that his final days would be very hard on his wife, so they had hired a home care nurse to help out during this extremely tough time.

The pastor arrived as the nurse was giving the dying man a sponge bath, changing his linen and bed clothes. He waited patiently in the den until she was through and beckoned him into the room.

The pastor and the old man spent a good hour together as the old man prepared himself for exiting this world.

As the pastor left the bedroom, he was greeted by the man's wife.

"Thank you so very much for coming over," she said gratefully. "I know he had some things on his mind that he wanted to get right. He was a good man, but you know how things can just eat at us sometimes. He can be peaceful now."

"Yes," the minister replied. "He wanted to talk. I'm so grateful that I can serve in this way, please, I know that you may face some tough times soon. Please call whenever you need."

"I will," she agreed.

"Oh, by the way," he added, "I'm afraid I need to apologize for eating all those peanuts in the den while I was waiting."

"Oh, never you mind about that," she assured him. "Ever since I lost my teeth, all I can do is suck the chocolate off!"

submitted by Mark Gilroy

74

The Lawyer's Genie

A man walking along the beach found a bottle. When he rubbed it, lo and behold, a genie appeared.

"I will grant you three wishes," announced the genie. "But there is one condition. I am a lawyer's genie. That means that for every wish you make, every lawyer in the world gets the wish as well, only double."

The man thought about this for a while. "For my first wish, I would like twenty million dollars," he announced.

Instantly, the genie gave him a Swiss bank account number and assured the man that $20,000,000 had been deposited. "And every lawyer in the world has just received $40,000,000," the genie confirmed.
"I've always wanted a Ferrari," the man said.

"That's my second wish."

Instantly a Ferrari appeared. "And every lawyer in the world has just received two Ferraris," the genie added. "And what is your last wish?"

"Well," said the man, grinning, "I've always wanted to donate a kidney for transplant."

75

The Missing Person

A woman's husband was gone for several days when she decided she should go down to the police station and report it. Her dearest friend went with her for moral support.

"Can you describe your husband," the desk sergeant asked.

"Yes," the abandoned woman replied, "he's 35 years old, 6'2" tall and weighs 185 pounds. He has dark, wavy hair, an athletic build, he's polite and very good with children."

As they walked from the station, her friend exclaimed, "What were you talking about in there? Your husband is only 5'6", he's overweight, bald and he's mean to the kids!"

"I know," she answered quietly, "who wants him back?!"

76

The New Baby

A couple that I know just had a new baby. He was born on the first of the month, so they named him Bill.

77

The New Butcher

Then there was the guy up in the north country who went to trade school to become a butcher. After he completed his studies, he got a job in a small town butcher shop. This particular small town backed up against some prime hunting land and every hunting season, the entire town enjoyed a brisk and steady business from people all over the world who had come to hunt.

Well, it seems that this new butcher was on duty when a group of men came in from a very prosperous hunting outing. They had a big supply of moose that they had killed and they wanted the butcher to take care of the butchering.

It was a big job. And it took the new butcher several days before he had the task completed. He had all of the cuts packaged and marked, but to his dismay, there were still a lot of pieces of meat left over. In his limited experience, he had absolutely no idea where these pieces had come from or how they should be marked. So, he gathered up all of these unidentifiable pieces of moose meat and tossed them into a single bag. He marked it, *moosellaneous!*

78

The New Computer

Two men were examining the output of the new computer their office had recently acquired. Eventually one of them remarked, "Do you realize it would take 500 men 300 years to make a mistake this big?"

79

The New Ferrari

A hip young man bought a 1999 Ferrari GTO. It was the best and most expensive car available in the world, and it cost about $500,000. He took it out for a spin and while stopped for a red light, an old man on a moped (both looking about 90 years old) pulled up next to him.

The old man looked over the sleek, shiny surface of the car and asked, "What kind'a car ya' got there, Sonny?"

The young man replied, "It's a brand new 1999 Ferrari GTO. They cost about a half million dollars!"

"That's a lot of money," said the old man, shocked. "Why does it cost so much?"

"Because this car can do up to 320 miles an hour!"

stated the cool dude proudly.

The moped driver asked, "Can I take a look inside?"

"Sure," replied the owner.

So the old man poked his head in the window and looked around. Leaning back on his moped, the old man said, "Yep, that's a pretty nice car, all right!"

Just then the light changed so the guy decided to show the old man what his car could do. He floored it, and within 30 seconds the speedometer read 320 mph.

Suddenly, he noticed a dot in his rear view mirror. It seemed to be getting closer! He slowed down to see what it could be and suddenly. . .*whhhooooossshhh!* Something whipped by him, going much faster!

"What on Earth could be going faster than my Ferrari?!" the young man asked himself.

Then, ahead of him, he saw a dot coming toward him. *Whoooooosh!* It went by again, heading in the opposite direction! And it almost looked like the old man on the moped!

"Couldn't be," thought the guy. "How could a moped out run a Ferrari?!"

Again, he saw the dot in his rear view mirror! Whooooosh, ka-bbblaMMM! It plowed into the back of his Ferrari and demolished the rear end.

The young man jumped out, and it *was* the old man!!! Of course, the moped and the old man were hurting for certain. He ran up to the injured old guy and said, "You're badly hurt! Is there anything I can do for you?"

The old man moaned and replied, "Yes! Please unhook my suspenders from your side-view mirror!"

submitted by Larry James

<u>80</u>

The New Salesman

A keen country lad applied for a salesman's job at a city department store. In fact, it was the biggest store in the world, you could get anything there!

The boss asked him, "Have you ever been a salesman before?"

"Yes, I was a salesman in the country," said the lad.

The boss liked the cut of him and said, "You can start tomorrow and I'll come and see you when we close up."

The day was long and arduous for the young man, but finally 5 o'clock came around. The boss duly fronted up and asked, "How many sales did you make today?"

"One," said the young salesman.

"Only one?!" blurted the boss, "Most of my staff make 20 or 30 sales a day. How much was the sale worth?"

"Three hundred thousand dollars," said the young man.

"How did you manage that?" asked the flabber-gasted boss.

"Well," said the salesman, "this man came in and I sold him a small fish hook, then a medium hook and finally a really large hook. Then I sold him a small fishing line, a medium one and a huge big one. I asked him where he was going fishing and he said down the coast. I said he would probably need a boat, so I took him down to the boat depart-ment and sold him that twenty foot schooner with the twin engines. Then he said his Volkswagen probably wouldn't be able to pull it, so I took him to the car department and sold him the new Deluxe Cruiser."

The boss took two steps back and asked in aston-ishment, "You sold all that to a guy who came in for a fish hook?"

"No," answered the salesman "He came in to buy a

box of Tampons for his wife and I said to him, 'Your weekend's shot, you may as well go fishing.'"

submitted by Larry James

81

The Pink Panther

What happened when the Pink Panther stepped on the ant?

Dead ant, dead ant, dead ant, dead ant, dead ant.
(to the tune of the Pink Panther)

submitted by Kent Bowers

82

The Pit Bull

There was this one particular man who didn't much care for crime or electronic car alarms. He purchased and trained a pit bull terrier that he took everywhere as his "car alarm".

One day, he was traveling in a very nasty part of Philadelphia. He parked his car and started to head to a nearby address.

A street wise young man approached him. "Hey, mister," he hollered, "Ten bucks and I'll watch your car."

"Look, kid," the man answered, "You see that pit bull? I don't need anyone to look after my car. He does it for me!"

"Yeah?" the youth said, "Can the dog put out fires?"

"OK," came a quick reply, "Here's your ten bucks."

83

The Relatives

The Albertsons took vacation and decided to visit Mrs. Albertson's sister out in western Kansas. They hadn't seen each other in years and thought it about time.

Little Scotty Albertson was only five at the time. When, after the long drive they finally pulled into the relatives driveway, Mrs. Albertson's sister came running out to the car to greet the family. She was not an attractive woman.

"Oooooh!" squirmed little Scotty, "you sure are ugly."

Scotty's mother was aghast. She drew Scotty aside and said, "That was a terrible thing to say to your aunt. Now you march right over to her, young man, and tell her that you are sorry."

Little Scotty did what he was told. He stood up straight and walked directly over to his fearsome aunt. He stood before her and said, "Auntie, I am so sorry that you are so ugly."

84

The Rotary Club

Old Mike Clayton was sitting at home one morning before work. He was sipping his second cup of coffee when the phone rang. He answered it.

"Hello?" Mike asked.

"Mike, this is Jim Franston from Rotary. You know that I'm Rotarian of the Day today, and well, I just got a call and my speaker had to cancel. I know that you've had some speaking experience with your job, could I get you to fill in? I'd owe you, that's for sure!" came the panicked voice on the other end.

"Well, Jim, that surely does put you in a pickle! What was the topic?" Mike questioned.

"Sex," Jim answered. "The topic is *Sex in the Twenty First Century*, and we've got a booked slate!

Everyone wants to hear about it! There were absolutely no cancellations! In fact, we're supposed to have a whole bunch of visitors from some of the other groups in town! I just don't know what to do!"

"Jim," Mike said. "I believe I can help you out. Rest easy, I'll fill in."

"Bless you," Jim said.

That noon Mike gave his speech. It was a fantastic oration, with so much humor, it was hilarious! Mike received a standing ovation!

He went home that evening and told his wife that he had filled in for the speaker that day and received a standing ovation. To his surprise, his wife asked him what he had talked about. Mike wasn't certain that he wanted his wife to know that he had been talking about sex with all these other guys, and he didn't know how his wife would take it.

"Skiing," Mike lied. "I talked about down hill skiing."

The wife looked puzzled.

That evening, Mrs. Clayton went to the store, she had some grocery shopping to do and just about in the cereal aisle, who should she run into but Jim Franston from Rotary. Jim went on and on about what a great job Mike had done that day.

Mrs. Clayton finally broke in to his accolades, "I just don't understand how he could be such an expert. He's only done it once, he fell down and his hat blew off!"

85

The Security Guards

There were these two security guards out at the airport. They weren't the best of security guards, if you know what I mean. It's not like they were police officers doing extra duty. They didn't even attend any kind of class or school. Somehow they just ended up as security guards.

This one fine day, they were watching some planes land and take off. The first one, Jim, kept shaking his head and muttering to himself, "I don't understand it. I just don't understand it."

Finally, his buddy, Ray, turned and said to him, "Jim, what are you talking about? Just what is it that you don't understand?"

"Ray," Jim said, still wagging his head back and forth, "I just don't understand how anyone can hijack a plane. I mean, how do you steal something so blooming big?!"

"Jim, you fool," Ray answered. "They don't steal it down here on the ground. They wait until it's way up in the air, when it's only this *(holding his forefinger and thumb about a half inch apart)* big!"

86

The Stolen Crown Jewels

One winter day, a French Count and an accomplice succeeded in stealing all of the Queen's many jewels.

The King was led by a number of small clues to the Count. After many days of being beaten and tortured, the King was able to secure a confession from the Count, but still, the Count would not tell who had helped him with the heist. Finally in exasperation, the King demanded that the Count tell, "Tell me who your partner is in this crime, tell me, or it is off to the chopping block with you and you shall lose your head!"

Still the count was silent. The count was led away to the chopping block. As he lay his head across the huge oaken stump, he was given one more chance to tell the King who had helped him. And, once more, the stubborn Count refused.

The executioner raised his giant axe. Up, up it went, it reached its peak, and the great weapon began to fall.

"I'll tell! I'll tell!" shouted out the Count. But it was too late, the axe fell and the Count's bloody head bearing a most terrified expression rolled from the oaken stump and into the waiting basket.

The King was forlorn, if he had just waited another few moments he could have had his answer. But, now, he would never know.

The moral of the story? *Don't hatch your Counts before they chicken, of course!*

87

The Texas Town

Then there's those two women who are driving through Texas in order to get to South Padre Island. It is nearing noon time, they're hungry and so they begin to look for a place to stop and have lunch. They travel a bit further and then see a sign that says: Mexia 5 miles.

The one driving, Theresa, says, "Oh, look Cathy, Mexia is only five miles."

Cathy responds, "Where? I believe the town is pronounced 'Muh-hey-uh'."

For the next five miles they argue over how to pronounce the name of the little place. When they arrive, and pull into one of the local fast food places, they are still arguing over how to pronounce the name of this town.

They exit their car and walk into the eatery. They

sit down in a booth and look over the selections.

The waitress approaches to take their order. "May I help you?" the young girl asks the two traveling maidens.

"Yes," Theresa replies, "We've been having an argument over how to pronounce something. Can you tell us the name of where we are and, please, say it for us slowly?"

The waitress looks puzzled for a moment, shrugs and says, "DARE-REE-QUEEN."

88

The Thousand Year Old man

Perhaps you remember that not too long ago there was a one thousand year old Viking who was found frozen high up in the mountains. He was found in a glacier and had been apparently on some sort of trek. He was dressed in a traveler's fashion and wore the garb of an ancient Norseman. A team of scientists brought the body down out of the hills and he was eventually taken to the British Museum. The body had been kept frozen all through the transportation process. After a complete inspection, many photographs, drawings and measurements, it was determined that the body would be thawed, whereas a number of experiments could then take place on tissues and vital organs.

A slow and careful thawing process took place, and to the amazement of all, and in fact, it had to have been a miracle, as the thawing reached a certain stage, the huge Viking's heart began to beat.

Yes, it was a miracle! The heart was beating, blood was surging through the vein's of the ancient warrior and respiration began! The huge chest was moving in and out in the slow and steady process of breathing!

And, yet, there were no brain waves! How could this be?! No one had an answer, and they all hoped that, perhaps with another miracle, perhaps the brain might start functioning.

The old Viking was shipped by helicopter transport to the United States where he was to be seen by the world renown neurologist, Dr. Jonathan Walker. Dr. Walker examined the felled warrior and immediately began to perform steps that the world hoped might help the Viking to regain consciousness. Dr. Walker and his team worked day and night for many weeks, but to no avail. After 102 days, the team gave up. The brain simply could not function.

Yes, you can take a Norse to Walker, but you can't make him think.

89

The Traffic Stop

The couple was pulled over in their BMW by the State Trooper.

"Excuse me, sir," the officer said, "I need to see your license, your registration and your insurance verification."

"What seems to be the problem, officer," the man asked.

"Sir, the reason that I stopped you is that I clocked you at 75m.p.h. and the speed limit is only 65," the officer explained.

"Oh, my," the man replied, "there must be some mistake, I'm sure that I was only doing 60!"

"Oh, Harold!" the wife cried out, "You know darn well that you have been doing nearly 80 all along here!"

"Hmmm," the officer mused. "I'm also citing you for a broken tail light."

"But officer!" Harold pleaded, "surely you can let that go, I didn't even know it was broken, it must have happened just last night!"

"Harold!" the wife chastised, "You quit your lying! You've known for over a week that that light was broken!"

"I thought so," the trooper continued, "finally, sir, I am going to have to cite you for not wearing your seat belt."

"Oh, now, officer," Harold spoke up, "I only undid it as you approached the car!"

"Harold," the wife chided, "You never wear your seat belt."

"Margaret," Harold exploded, "You need to keep your *!(>!*<) %#@!&! mouth shut!"

The officer leaned forward, he looked into the car, across Harold, and at the reprimanded wife. "Ma'am," he asked, "Does your husband always speak to you so harshly?"

"Oh, no!" Margaret answered. "Only when he's been drinking!"

90

The Train Ride

I was traveling by train from Gothenburg to Stockholm, and fell into a conversation with a couple of local guys. One of them, Sven, was a typically mild and rather laid-back Swede, but the other, Olf, was more of an individualist. He was on his way back from a Fifties revival weekend in England, and was dressed the part; black leather jacket, really tight blue jeans, skin tight white t-shirt, a ducktail hairstyle, the complete *Teddy* look. He was getting fed up with the odd looks and re-marks from his fellow passengers and was begin-ning to get quite offensive in his replies.

I bought them both a beer, but no sooner had we cracked open the cans and begun to drink them, then Olf sputtered, shoved down the window and hurled his can out. "Bloody foul rubbish!" he shouted, "why doesn't this line stock decent Dan-ish Railways lager?"

"Goodness," I remarked to Sven, "he seems to have firm opinions on this!"

"Oh yes", said Sven, *"Rude Olf the Ted knows train beer."*

91

The Tree Feller

This good old boy walked into a hardware store and started looking at the chain saws.

"May I help you?" the store clerk asked.

"Welp, I'm lookin' for me a good saw," he answered. "What kind of a price do these run?"

"Well, sir," the clerk began, "these models run from $125 on up to this top of the line model that goes for $450."

"$450!" the old boy exclaimed. "What! Are they made of gold?!"

"No, sir, but it's guaranteed for life, and for the type of trees that we find around in these parts, you can cut down, oh, upwards to about fifty trees in one day with this little beauty," the merchant stated.

The vendor smiled at the potential customer, then he picked up the little beast and put it into the waiting hands of the old boy.

"Feel how balanced it is, notice the fine craftsmanship. This is more than a tool, it is an excellent example of precision equipment," he continued.

The old guy beamed. "It does feel nice, it must be worth it if it can cut down that many trees in a day. Son, I believe you have just sold me."

The old man paid his cash and drove off.

Two days later the old fellow pulled up in front of the store. He got out of his truck and from out of the back end he pulled out that brand new chain saw. He proceeded to walk into the hardware store and look for the clerk with which he had done business two days prior. He scowled.

"Hey, there, boy!" he hollered, "I need to have a word with you!"

"Yes, sir," replied the young man smartly, "how can I help you?"

"This here chain saw that you sold me the other

day ain't no good! I worked like a dog all day long yesterday from sun up 'til past sun down and I'll be danged if'n I couldn't get no more than three trees felled. Where in the heck you came up with that number of fifty trees a day, I sure don't know!" The man was quite angry.

The salesman knew that one must get an angry customer away from the other customers in the store, so he suggested, "Why don't we go out back and take a look? Maybe something is wrong with it?"

The smart young man put his hand on the disgruntled workers shoulder and the two proceeded out the back of the store.

Outside, the salesman asked the old man, "Do you mind if I take a look?"

"Go right ahead, I'm tired of carrying the piece of junk!" came the quick answer.

The tool vendor looked at the machine, he checked the gas, gave it a little choke and pulled on the starting cord. The machine quickly flew into action with the noisy whirrr of a small gasoline engine.

"HEY!" the old man cried, "What's that noise?"

92

The Twilight Zone

Why does the Twilight Zone smell so bad?

Doo doo, doo doo, doo doo, doo doo.*
(* of course, to that theme!)

93

The Ugly Girl

A very homely young woman made an appointment with a psychiatrist. She walked into his office and asked, "Doctor, I am so depressed and lonely. I don't have any friends, no man will come near me, and everybody laughs at me. Can you help me accept my ugliness?"

"Oh, certainly, miss, I'm sure I can," the psychiatrist answered. "Please, just go over and lie face down on that couch."

94

The Wedding

The little boy was attending his very first wedding, ever, in his whole life. He was taking everything in and you could see his little mind just working away. After a time, he tugged on his mother's sleeve and asked, "Mommy, how come that lady is dressed all in white?"

"Well, son," the mother tried to answer, "'that lady' is called the bride. The bride is dressed all in white because she is so happy. This is the happiest day of her life."

The young lad thought for a moment and asked, "How come that man is all dressed in black?"

95

Those Drunk Drivers

Then there were those two drunks who had been out all night drinking. They were driving down the highway when suddenly one of them noticed that there were the flashing lights of a patrol car behind them. The driver started to pull over to the side of the road.

"What are we going to do?" asked the worried passenger.

The driver said calmly, "Don't worry! Just do exactly as I tell you! Quickly peel two labels off of two of those beer bottles, hurry! Slide the bottles under the seat and now stick one label on your forehead. Now put the other one on mine, now hurry! Okay, now let me do all of the talking! We'll be okay!

The driver's inebriated buddy quickly did as he was told. He had just finished sliding all the bottles under the seat when the officer approached the car, shining his flashlight in across the both of them.

"Good evening, gentlemen," the officer started. "May I see your license and proof of insurance."

"Yes, sir," the driver replied. He got out the two documents and handed them to the uniformed officer.

"Have you gentlemen been drinking this evening?" asked the policeman.

"Oh, no, sir!" the driver responded without hesitation. "Not at all."

"Are you sure?" probed the cop. "I noticed that you were weaving quite a bit back there. It seemed that you were having some trouble staying within your lane."

"Sir, we haven't had a drop this evening," the driver assured him. "No, sir, not a drop! I promise!"

The officer shined his flashlight once again across the two guys. He shined it on one of the drunk's foreheads and then across to the other and back again.

"Fellows," the patrolman asked, "just what are those things on your foreheads?"

"Oh, that! That's easy!" claimed the drunk. "You see, we're both alcoholics and we're on the patch!"

96

Trouble

A young man was speeding his hot red sports car down the main street of a small Oklahoma town. He hadn't gone very far before one of the town's finest pulled him over.

"Boy," he said to the young visitor. "I'm tired of you college kids driving through here in your fancy, smancy cars as though we didn't have no local laws a'tall."

"But officer. . . ," the young man tried to interject.

"Shut up, boy," the local continued. "You think you're such a hot shot, I think I'll just let you cool your heels a bit in jail. We'll just see how smart you are sittin' in one of our cells."

"But officer. . ." the detainee tried once more.

"Boy, don't you even try to say another word, if

you know what's good for you," the officer threatened. "You just shut up, you can tell your story to the chief."

A couple of hours later, the officer approached the cell. The young man was lying down on the cot, looking mournfully up at the ceiling.

The officer said, "You know, kid, the chief don't normally take to kids speedin' through our town. You're lucky today, though. Today his daughter is getting married, that's where he's at, he's at the wedding right now. The chief will be in a good mood when he gets back."

The boy sat up and looked at the patrol officer. "Don't count on it," he replied. "I'm the groom."

97

True Love

Then there was that guy who met that girl in a revolving door. They've been going around together ever since.

■ ■ ■ ■ ■ ■ ■ ■ ■

The other night, they were sitting on the couch watching TV.

The girl said, "Please, say you love me. Say you love me."

"You love me," he replied.

98

What Do You Get?

What do you get when you cross a Jehovah's Witness with a Unitarian?

Somebody who knocks on your door for no apparent reason!

99

What Is It?

What's black, shriveled and hangs from the ceiling?

An incompetent electrician.

100

What?

What happens once in a minute, twice in a moment and never in a thousand years.

The letter M.

submitted by Jimmy Sutherland.

101

Who's On First

My wife and I had a huge argument the other day. It was right in the middle of the World Series and she came in and started yelling all over the place.

She was mad because she said that all I was interested in was baseball. She said all I ever talked about was baseball. She said all I ever watched on TV was baseball. She said that the only thing I cared about was baseball.

I told her she was way off base.

102

Wise, Powerful & Rich

"Who is wise? He that learns from everyone. Who is powerful? He that governs his passions. Who is rich? He who is content. Who is that? Nobody."

Benjamin Franklin

103

Woman Driver

This woman was driving along through the countryside with her best friend. They came around a blind corner and saw some utility men climbing up a pole.

"Those fools," the woman remarked to her companion. "They must think I've never driven before!"

104

The School Boy

Little Johnny was in first grade when his father took him to be circumsized.

The next day, his teacher noticed him squirming and moving around in his seat. "Are you okay," she asked.

"I got circumcized yesterday," Johnny explained.

"Would you like go to the office and call your mother?" the teacher asked sympathetically.

"Yes, ma'am," Johnny replied.

When he returned, his little pee-pee was sticking outside his trousers. "What did she say," asked the teacher.

"She said stick it out 'til noon, then she'll come get me!"

submitted by Mardell Finsel

John Irvin

John Irvin resides in Tulsa, Oklahoma *(where everything is O.K.)* and is the president of Lifestyle Enhancement Services (LES), a successful motivational and consulting business.

LES offers keynotes, seminars and workshops that are designed to enhance conferences, conventions, annual meetings, trainings and special events. In fact, LES will make any meeting a special event!

John, a graduate of the University of Tulsa, has been creating "playful opportunities" for personal and professional growth for over twenty years. Today, as the creator of Hilarity Therapy® Programs, John shares from his work in corporate training, leisure sciences, mental health and health and wellness education the message that each of us has the ability to enjoy life more.

John says, "all work and no play make Jack *(and Jill)* suicidal!"

John Irvin is a member of the American Association for Therapeutic Humor, the National Speakers Association, the Oklahoma Speakers Association, the American Society for Training and Development, the Humor and Health Institute, the Association for Experiential Education, Project Adventure, Inc., and the International Jugglers Association.

*For more information on John Irvin
and his programs contact:*

Cindy Irvin, P.M.S.
(Professional Marketer of Spouse)
LifestyleEnhancement Services
Post Office Box 4397
Tulsa, Oklahoma 74159-0397

888-997-PHUN
or e-mail us at
jmi1953@ionet.net